THE GREEN VAULT

THE GREEN VAULT

An Introduction

State Art Collections in Dresden

Figure on the front
fly-leaf:
Valuables Room of the Green Vault
in Dresden Castle,
southern wall, in 1904 –
The furnishings have survived

Figure on the end
fly-leaf:
Jewel Room of the Green Vault
in Dresden Castle,
northern wall, right-hand side, in 1904 –
The furnishings were destroyed in 1945

Ninth edition 1990
Published by:
Staatliche Kunstsammlungen Dresden
GDR 8012 Dresden, P. O. B. 450, BN 93677903
JG 71/15/90 (70/89)
Text: Joachim Menzhausen
Catalogue: Werner Kiontke
Translation: Hartmut Angermüller
Layout: Lothar Ziratzki, Conrad Berge
Printed by:
Grafische Werke Zwickau III/29/1
Photos:
Klaus G. Beyer, Weimar
J. Willsberger (pp. 104, 105)
Museum of History of the Town of Dresden
(Fly-leaves)
© Staatliche Kunstsammlungen Dresden 1977

01500

The Green Vault (Grünes Gewölbe) was the treasure-house of the electors of Saxony. It contains more than 3,000 works of art in gold, silver, precious stones, ivory, ebony and amber, and also in glass, brass and bronze. It is the largest collection of precious objects in Europe. About half of its stock is now on display, with the different groups of objects represented to varying degrees, e. g. most of the large stock of ivory, bronze and rock-crystal is still in storage facilities, while nearly all jewellery is on view.

Why are these treasures so numerous? Why are they of such great artistic value? A look at the Saxon electorate's economic and political importance and its history will explain. Silver deposits were discovered in the hills of Saxony at the end of the twelfth century. The subsequent period saw a rapid expansion of mining; and the electorate became one of Europe's major exporters not only of silver, but also of tin, iron, copper, cobalt and valuable stones like serpentine and jasper. As early as the late Middle Ages Saxony had a bourgeoisie that controlled a flourishing industry. Towns which are insignificant today built churches as large as those of the powerful Hanseatic towns in the North and exceeding them in the splendour of their interior decorations. In the market-places of their towns sixteenth-century burghers put up townhalls which made aristocratic castles appear modest in comparison. It was by no means accidental that European Protestantism had its origins in Saxony and that the electorate remained its most powerful exponent for a long time.

Therefore the Saxon electors of the House of Wettin took a considerable interest in economic affairs and came to be very learned in them. They also had an unusual ability to judge the performance of craftsmen. This is shown by the fact that

Elector Augustus established the Dresden Art Chamber (Dresdener Kunstkammer) in 1560. The Art Chamber was an all-round museum representing all the branches of technology and science known at the time, with paintings and sculptures assigned a subordinate róle only. Important parts of the stock of the Green Vault were later taken from this collection, especially valuable works in gilded silver combined with natural produce like ostrich-eggs, coconuts, sea-shells and corals, astronomical clocks and turnery pieces in ivory.

In addition to the Art Chamber, Dresden Royal Castle had a strong-room, the Secret Depository (Geheime Verwahrung), as it was called. Originally, the Secret Depository had just one room on the ground floor; later on, two adjacent rooms were added. The three rooms were regarded as the most fire- and burglar-proof in the castle. They had outer walls more than 80 inches thick, windows that were protected by heavy lattices and iron shutters, and arched ceilings. Fire could never reach the government securities, the cash reserves and the precious objects which were stored there. Winding stairs hidden inside the internal walls led up to the rooms in which the elector lived.

The first, original room was painted green; and this may have been the reason why the inhabitants of the castle referred to it colloquially as the green vault, a term which was to become generally accepted later on. The first treasure-house museum was set up in these rooms in 1723—24. Its stock was taken from the Secret Depository and the Art Chamber, and partly also from the Silver Chamber, the place where the elector's table silver was stored and looked after.

More walls were broken down between 1727 and 1730 to add another four show-rooms and a vestibule with small adjoining rooms. Entry was now from there. These changes created something that is amazing, interesting and noteworthy even by today's standards.

Ever since groups of men started living in fairly well-organized sedentary communities they have had treasure-houses to store worshipping gear, the insignia of rulers, precious metal or money reserves and even special weapons. They were in every case accessible only to the highest priests or the rulers and their senior officials. It was therefore most remarkable that one of the world's richest secret vaults was opened to the public and converted into a museum. What is more, the museum was presumably the first of the type that is now found all over the world; for it did not only have show-rooms, but also a foyer with a cloakroom, a work-room for the official in charge, storage facilities and even an entrance of its own. All passages leading to it from inside the castle had been walled up, probably because the existence of only one approach is essential to the safety of a treasure-house. But the point that is of importance to us today is that this museum was an isolated functional organism, which all museums are today.

The establishment of the museum was part of a wider effort to reorganize art collecting. Those years also saw the foundation of Kupferstich-Kabinett (a collection of copper-plate engravings), the picture gallery, the porcelain collection and natural science collections.

Fig. on the opposite page
Relief plate showing the apostles John and Paul Byzantine, mid-1oth cent., ivory, silver, partly gilded, 9⁷/₈ × 5¹/₄ inches

Fig. on pp. 8–9
Three gryphon claws, horn in settings of gilded silver, German, late 14th till mid-15th cent., 12 × 16; 8⁷/₈ × 9⁷/₈; 9³/₄ × 9 inches

Most of their stocks came from the Art Chamber as well. There may have been two main reasons for calling in an army of scientists, restorers, architects, artists and craftsmen to do skilled and therefore costly work for a number of years. Ruling Elector Augustus, who was to be known as Augustus the Strong later on, had himself elected King of Poland in 1697. The Kingdom of Poland, together with economically powerful Saxony, was an important political force in Europe at that time. The monarch was seeking to turn the two countries into an East European great power—a political speculation that was subsequently to evaporate like a dream. But in those days he saw a need for converting ancient Dresden, which had been the slightly provincial centre of his electorate, into a modern European royal capital.

This required museums. When travelling in his youth, the king had seen specialized collections in the large old centres of power and art in Europe. Compared with them, the Art Chamber was based on obsolete and very vague concepts. A superabundance of works of art, natural products, scientific instruments and technological gear had been crammed into it in wild disarray, probably causing a lot of harm to one another. So he was both furthering his own political ends and following his wide-ranging personal inclinations when he turned that conglomeration of objects into specialized collections. To increase the glory of his newly won kingship, he ordered all the cultural possessions that the House of Wettin had amassed for generations to be arranged in long galleries according to the academic principles of thematic and historical categorization which the beginning era of Enlightenment had been evolving. A combination of both thematic and historical considerations helped display the material on hand in the most meaningful and intelligent manner. The arrangement chosen at the time was so ingenious that it has been retained to this day; the inventories compiled by expert court officials in those days are still used whenever some collection is being prepared for display. It is true, however, that the stock of the Green Vault stimulated the imagination and creativity of those officials in the strongest possible manner to find an arrangement that would be ideally suited to glorify the absolute monarchy. The chief architect employed for the purpose was Pöppelmann, who was the builder of the Zwinger, a famous Baroque building of the Dresden court. He had the wall panels immediately below the arches of the vaults covered with carved, varnished and gilded ornaments and panes of plate-glass, with a decorative array of brackets in front of them. Rows of gilded tables were placed in front of the panels of the walls. The columns were covered with pier-glasses, the floors and door jambs were cut from Saxon marble. The most important works of art were placed on the marble tops of the tables; and other very valuable pieces were put on the lower brackets. This created the two major viewing levels of the exhibition. The predominantly ornamental works were placed on a third level, the upper part of the walls up to about 13 feet, adding to the general impression the display makes on the visitor. The exhibits doubled optically in the mirrors and multiplied in the pier-glasses on the opposite walls and columns. The lavish profusion of three-dimensionality which was to be found in the Zwinger was here reproduced with other means and fused to create a highly artistic, colourful ensemble of interior decoration. The best artists of the court were lending a hand. Court Sculptor Benjamin Thomae carved the tables and brackets. One of his apprentices and assistants was Johann Joachim Kändler, who was to become the creator of European porcelain style and a famous designer at the factory in the town of Meissen near Dresden making the famous Dresden porcelain. Court varnishers Martin Schnell and Christian Reinow, who are now known as masters of Saxon varnished furniture making, varnished the furniture of whole rooms. Gold etchings were placed behind panes of glass that were covered with red and blue varnish. These mirror-rooms of Saxony's treasure-house soon became well-known all over Europe; and a travelling writer who was very popular at the time described them as the most beautiful spot on earth.

Apart from the insignificant damage done by wars, and several periods of restoration, the Green Vault looked like this all along until 1942. Certain additions from other Dresden museums, a purchase here and a purchase there, and some losses due to sales were never important enough to affect the collection substantially. But the collection entered the most difficult period of its history, a period full of gravest hazards, when the Western Allies were stepping up the bombardment of German towns in 1942 in the wake of savage attacks of Nazism on he nations of Europe. Instruction was therefore given to evacuate the collection to the ancient mountain-fortress of Königstein not far away in Saxon Switzerland. On February 13th, 1945 the whole of downtown Dresden was devastated in the heaviest air-raid ever flown by the united Anglo-American air forces in World War Two. The Royal Castle was burnt out. Only those rooms which were considered safest even in the sixteenth century remained on the whole undamaged. Five of the original eight rooms of the Green Vault were the only ones in the old part of Dresden

not to be destroyed in that night-attack. Luckily enough. They are some of the best and most beautiful rooms of that admirable Dresden period of European Baroque.

Most of the interior decoration left of the Green Vault is now stored at the Dresden Institute of Monument Conservation. But parts of the Silver Room and the entire Corner Room, which is one of the most exquisite rooms, have already been moved back to their original places on the ground floor of the western wing of the castle. You will now find the offices and show-rooms of the Architects Union of the German Democratic Republic there. — Yet the magnificent marble-topped tables, most of them gilded, and also the display wall with its silver gear in the first room of our exhibition and the display wall with ivory pieces in the second are from Pöppelmann's original furnishings, too. We allowed them to determine the character of the treasure-house when we were furnishing it again.

On the day Hitler's Reich surrendered, the German commandant of Königstein Fortress gave all the keys to the most senior of the high French officers who had been held captive there, including the key of the casemate where the treasures of the Green Vault were lying. A special detachment of the Soviet Army which had been instructed to salvage the Dresden art treasures learned about their whereabouts only a few days later. A guard was put at the entrance of the casemate, and before long the treasures were all transferred to Moscow to be deposited in the safes of the USSR's Ministry of Finance. Soviet art historians were called in to rig them up and look after them. This was how they were saved from the dangers and confusions at the end of the war. The collection is one of the few museums of the former German Reich which outlasted the fascist war virtually without loss. Like the exhibits of other art museums, it was returned to the government of the GDR in 1958; and as soon as May 8th, 1959 the first exhibition was opened at Albertinum. The present new exhibition was opened on the 25th anniversary of the GDR in 1974, the year of the 250th anniversary of the Green Vault. Its museological arrangement does justice to the value of the art collection and meets the expectations of steadily increasing numbers of visitors. It is a vivid example of how artistic heritage can best be received, a question which is now being widely discussed in the GDR.

Fig. on the opposite page
Christ's Family Tree, "Viper Tree",
presumably Nuremberg, around 1500,
silver, partly gilded,
shark teeth,
h 7³/₄ inches

The Green Vault does not contain many
medieval works of art, although enormous
amounts of silver were mined in Saxony
after the end of the twelfth century. The
reason is that the upheavals of the
Early Bourgeois Revolution and the subsequent period brought about the destruction
not only of the incredibly large church
treasures—because they had all been used
in Catholic worship—but also of secular
silver—because its Gothic forms were then
thought to be irreconcilable with the new
outlook on art. Only those of the treasures
of the Saxon electors appear to have
been spared whose original religious
purpose was not too obvious or which did
not contain enough precious metal to
make destruction worthwhile (figures above
and on pp. 15 and 8/9).

Fig. on the left
Three Gothic rock-crystal vessels
in settings of gilded silver,
partly enamelled:
small goblet,
presumably French, 14th cent., h 6³/₄ inches;
cup of Queen Hedwig of Poland,
French, presumably 14th cent., the setting
Cracow Court Workshop, before 1399,
h 9¹/₂ inches;
ewer,
French, second half of the 14th cent.,
setting 15th cent., h 8¹/₄ inches

Fig. above
Three Gothic vessels:
vessel with lid,
German, late 15th cent., amethyst and
agate, gilded silver, h 5¹/₂ inches;
goblet with lid,
Italian (?), around 1400,
jasper, copper and bronze gilded,
h 8⁷/₈ inches;
double driking-cup,
serpentine, gilded silver,
presumably Nuremberg, around 1500,
h 6¹/₈ inches

This rosette-shaped pendant is one of the most beautiful pieces of jewellery left from the early sixteenth century. It may have been made in Nuremberg. The diamond rosette at its centre is most remarkable because India's grand moguls, who owned the only diamond mines known at the time, kept back all fairly large stones, so that for worthwhile coruscating effect several of the small stones available had to be pieced together. To obtain the angles required, craftsmen had to cut off more than 50 per cent of the stones, which, given the tools on hand at the time, was an exceedingly difficult, time-consuming and expensive job that only a very few highly skilled experts were able to do. That is why the richest dynasties alone could afford diamond rosettes. Lucas Cranach der Ältere put a very similar piece on his St. Catherine's Altar in 1506. (The altar is one of the exhibits of the Old Masters Picture Gallery). Since many wars were fought in those decades, pendants showing St. George, the dragon-killer, were very popular indeed. He was a saint of the soldiers. He was usually depicted as a knight on horseback. But the two sword fighters (Fig. on page 18, right-hand upper corner), who are made of set diamonds, are images of the saint as well. They are fragments of pendants. Tiny though they are, the figures have strength and clarity of movement, which reveals the high standards reached in all art forms of German Renaissance.

Fig. above
Rosette pendant,
presumably Nuremberg, early 16th cent.,
gold, diamonds, rubies, emeralds,
$2 \times 1^3/_4$ inches

Fig. in the left-hand upper corner
Pendant with St. George,
Dutch (?), around 1500,
mother-of-pearl, gilded silver,
dia 2⅝ inches

Fig. in the right-hand upper corner
Two parts of pendants,
German, early 16th cent.,
gold, flat and pointed diamond stones:
St. George with scimitar,
face enamelled white, h 1¾ inches;
St. George with sword,
face in mother-of-pearl, sword blade
in iron, h 2 inches

Fig. on the opposite page
Rings,
gold, partly enamelled:
ring with death's-head, alleged to have
been owned by Martin Luther,
German, early 16th cent.;
ring with turquoise,
made for Elector Christian II,
presumably Dresden, early 17th cent.;
Martin Luther's signet-ring, with cornelian,
Augsburg, around 1530;
ring with jaspagate,
from the possessions of Ph. Melanchthon,
German, first half of the 16th cent.;
ring with sapphire, alleged to have been
owned by Elector Johann Friedrich
of Saxony, German, around 1540;
ring with pyramid-shaped diamonds,
German, around 1570–80

Until the Battle at Mühlberg in 1547 Wittenberg was the Saxon electorate's capital. Luther, who was teaching at the town's university, launched the Reformation there. Politically, the Duchy of Saxony, which was ruled from the town of Freiberg, a centre of mining, was of secondary importance. This will explain why the additions made to the collection in the decades following the year 1500 were not numerous; they were valuable, though.

Here is a strange eighteenth-century story: In 1508 Augustin Kesenbrot, from Olomouc, who was Chancellor of the Kingdom of Hungary, presented a gold bowl (Fig. on the opposite page), into which antique coins had been set, to the Danubian Literary Society, an organization of humanists founded to cultivate arts and sciences. This is what the inscription says that is engraved on it. It is reported that after the chancellor's death the bowl got into his funeral church in Olomouc, where it fell into the hands of looting Turkish soldiers in the seventeenth century. Russian troops of Czar Peter the Great found it in 1696, when they were storming their way into Asov on the Black Sea, which was a Turkish fortress at that time. Saxon Chancellor Count Beichlingen bought it for Augustus the Strong and brought it to Dresden, relating this story. The story is unverifiable; only its beginning and its end are certain.

After the Battle at Mühlberg in 1547, when the united Protestant armed forces of the Schmalkalden League were beaten by the army of Emperor Charles V, the electoral dignity passed from the Wittenberg Ernestinian line of the House of Wettin to its Dresden and Freiberg Albertinian line. At that time Dresden was being turned into a powerful fortified royal capital. In a newly built wing of the castle the Secret Depository of the Green Vault was set up to house the most beautiful works of art of famous European artist-craftsmen: oriental basins and ewers in mother-of-pearl, which were given silver settings in Nuremberg; enamelled gear of unique artistry, which only a few family businesses in Limoges in Southern France knew how to make; and rock-crystal vessels in settings of gold, enamel and precious stones, which only few craftsmen in Milan were capable of cutting and designing.

In those days, when food was eaten not with forks yet, but with spoons and knives, unless the diners used their hands, well-to-do families had servants pass them washing gear at table. Water smelling sweet with attar of roses was poured from ewers over outstretched hands into basins. Therefore the Green Vault contains a large number of sets of basins and ewers made in the decades around 1600.

Translation of page 22:

On the Green Vault

The eye will never see enough,
Says Solomon in his Proverbs.
Oh, that he never saw Dresden!
He would certainly have altered,
If not deleted, this sentence.
Looking at this Royal Treasure
That the green room glistens with,
The eye will see enough,
Never yearning to see again.

By Daniel Wilhelm Triller, 1732

Fig. above
Gold bowl
of Sodalitas Litteraria Danubiana,
with Roman coins,
South East German, 1508, dia 7¹/₄ inches

Fig. on p. 23
Rose-water basin and ewer,
the setting from Nuremberg, 1530–40,
mosaic of mother-of-pearl, gilded silver,
basin: dia 22 inches; ewer: h 11¹/₂ inches

Fig. on pp. 24–25
Basin and ewer in Limoges enamel,
Limoges, late 16th cent., enamel on copper,
basin: 16¹/₄ × 21³/₄ inches
ewer: h 11 inches

Über das grüne Gewölbe:

Das Auge sieht sich nimmer satt:
Sagt Salomo in seinen Sprüchen.
Ach, daß er Dresden nicht gesehen hat!
Vermuhtlich hätt er diesen Satz
Geändert, wo nicht ausgestrichen:
Hier an dem Königlichen Schatz,
Womit das grüne Zimmer pranget,
Sieht sich das Auge völlig satt,
Daß es nichts mehr zu sehn verlanget.

Von Daniel Wilhelm Triller, 1732

APOCAL XVII

Fig. above
Basin in mother-of-pearl and ewer,
by Elias Geyer,
Leipzig, 1611–13,
mother-of-pearl, gilded silver,
wooden core, black putty,
basin: dia 23³/₄ inches; ewer h 13³/₄ inches

Fig. on p. 28
Box for writing utensils,
by Wenzel Jamnitzer, Nuremberg, 1562,
silver, partly gilded,
enamel, rock-crystal and ebony,
12¹/₄ × 9¹/₂ × 4³/₈ inches

Fig. on the opposite page
Large bottle with handle,
South German, around 1540,
gilded silver,
h 32 inches

Fig. on p. 29
Mount Calvary,
by Elias Lencker, Nuremberg, 1577,
gilded silver, wood,
pearl-oyster shells, monstrous pearls,
emeralds, turquoises, garnets,
26¹/₂ × 12¹/₄ × 7⁵/₈ inches

Wenzel Jamnitzer, from Nuremberg, was the best-known German goldsmith of the Renaissance. The little box for writing utensils on page 28 bears his stamp, marking it as made by him personally. He made the design for the jewel-case on pages 32/33 by Master Nicolaus Schmidt. The architecture-like basic forms of these boxes, many details of their ornamentation and the female figures resting on their lids clearly reveal the influence of Ancient Roman art, an influence that was of fundamental importance to entire European Renaissance. The intellectual efforts made in this period are reflected in the Latin rhyme in praise of the sciences which is inscribed on the tablet that the figure embodying philosophy at the top of the box holds in her hands. This shows that the court-nobility, for whom this piece was intended, was expected to know the Latin which was used by bourgeois humanists. When you press down a hidden spring in the box with a needle you can remove the wall at the feet of the figure. Inside you will find silk-lined ebony cases for all sorts of writing utensils and silver boxes for writing-sand and ink. Nearly all the techniques that a goldsmith was required to be conversant with at that time were used when the box was being made: hammering and soldering for the figure; making tiny casts from nature for the lid; founding, chasing, engraving and enamelling for the box; and, finally, fire gilding with a solution of gold and mercury.

Fig. on the opposite page
Communion-cup and wine can,
Nuremberg (?) and German,
around 1550–60,
gold, diamonds, gems, enamel,
h 7⅝, 6½ inches

Fig. below
Large jewel-case,
by Wenzel Jamnitzer
and Nicolaus Schmidt, Nuremberg,
around 1585,
silver, partly gilded,
mother-of-pearl, rock-crystal, emeralds,
garnets, amethysts, topazes,
coloured glass, wood,
$19^3/_4 \times 21^1/_4 \times 14^1/_4$ inches

Fig. on the opposite page
Part of the inner surface of the lid
of the large jewel-case
(silver, enamel, varnish, velvet, silk, pearls)

Fig. below
Jewel-case
(a part of it on the opposite page),
German, around 1600, ebony, gold, enamel,
$12^1/_2 \times 12^1/_2 \times 8^5/_8$ *inches*

IVSTICIA

When the fashion of the Spanish Empire was worn at virtually all European courts and had an influence even on the costumes of the middle classes, i.e. approximately from the mid-sixteenth century on, pendants of this kind began to be made; they resemble natural objects and are gold-enamelled. Formal clothes contrasted dark heavy colours with white lace. The face and the hands were the only places where skin showed. The rest of the body was hidden, and the human figure was adapted to a geometrical pattern. To emphasise and brighten up the dullness and sombreness of these clothes, colourful jewellery like that shown in the figures on pages 38, 39 and 41 was worn.

Czar Ivan the Terrible had this "Koffsh", an old Russian drinking-vessel, made from the gold found in the town of Polotsk when he was capturing it in 1563. At the beginning of the eighteenth century Czar Peter the Great gave it as a present to Polish King and Saxon Elector Augustus the Strong, his ally in the North European War. It was a truly princely gift, because it is one of the major master-pieces of the goldsmith's art of Russian Renaissance.

Fig. on p. 38
Pendant,
German and presumably French,
around 1560–70:
monogram pendant with the letters AA
(for Elector Augustus of Saxony and
Electress Anna),
pendant with cross rosette,
monogram pendant lettered A
(for Elector Augustus or Electress Anna)

Fig. on p. 39
Pendants,
St. George, Judgment of Paris, Siren,
Warrior's Head, German,
around 1570–1600, gold, diamonds, rubies,
one emerald, pearls, enamel

Fig. on p. 40
Necklaces,
German, third quarter of the 16th cent. till
around 1600, gold, enamel, lapis lazuli

Fig. on p. 41
Pendant,
German and Dresden, around 1600–11,
gold, diamonds, rubies, emeralds, enamel

Fig. on the opposite page
Drinking-vessel ("Koffsh") of
Czar Ivan the Terrible,
Moscow Court Workshop, after 1563,
gold, niello, sapphire, pearls,
19 inches

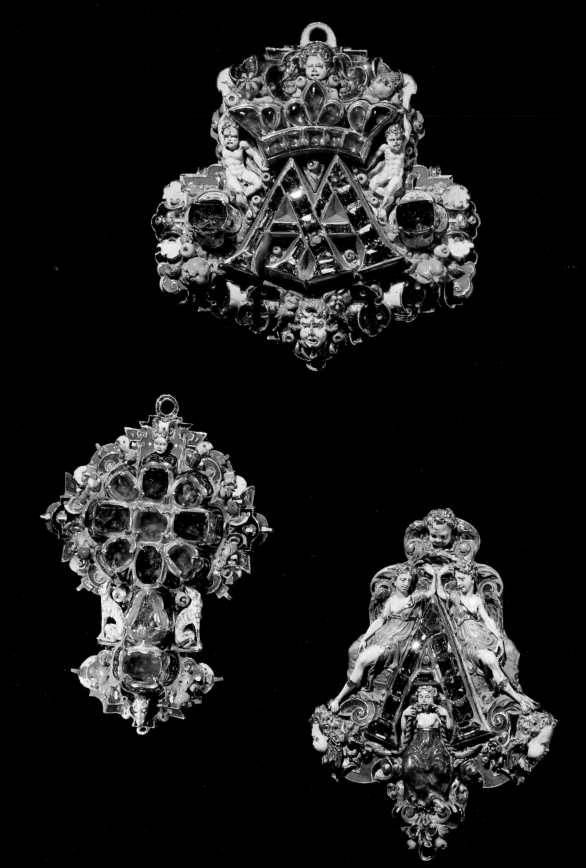

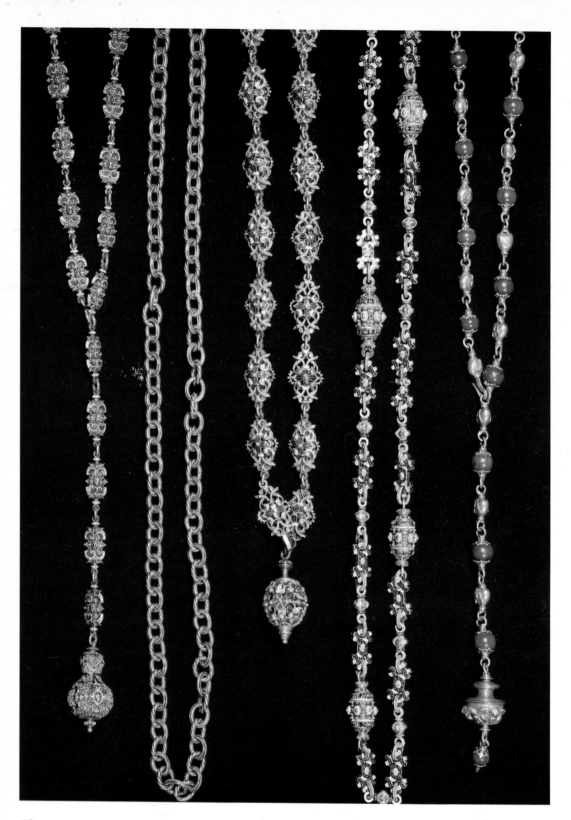

Fig. below
Disc with the coat-of-arms of Elector
Augustus, by Valentin Geitner,
Dresden 1586; spoon, presumably
Nuremberg, around 1600

Fig. on the opposite page
Reverse side of a mirror,
German, around 1600,
gold, enamel, h 7 inches, b 5⁷/₈ inches

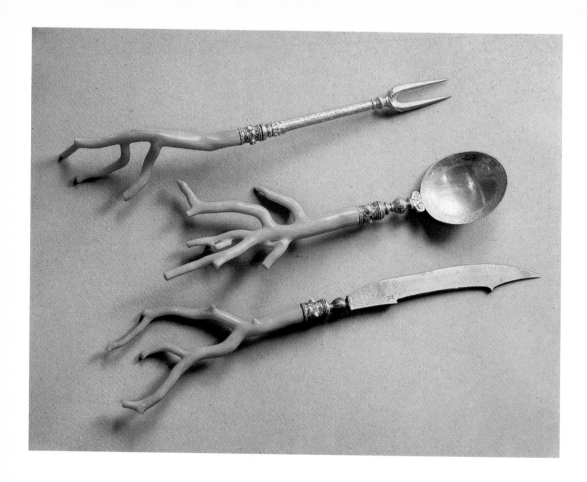

Drinking, the most wide-spread vice around 1600, produced just as many forms of objects as smoking does today, when we have a variety of holders, pipes, ash-trays and lighters. Coffee and tea were not known yet. Whenever people met socially they drank liquor, wine and beer. Strength, courage and skill were tested to add to the general merry-making: a person who had emptied an elephant was considered as having subdued the animal; to defeat an ostrich you needed to take off his head, catch with your mouth the beverage spouting intermittently from his narrow throat, and avoid giving a start when as soon as the animal came to be held at a certain large angle, his wings, which were suspended from hinges, suddenly hit your eyes; hunters drank from Daphne the virgin, who, pursued by Apollo, had been saved by being changed into a laurel tree. The devices invented were numberless; those used at court were made of silver, and those used by peasants, of cheap glass. In the Thirty Years' War a priest, giving a penitential sermon, fulminated against people drinking from monks and nuns, monkeys and clerics, and even from the devil.

Fig. on the opposite page
Set of knife, fork and spoon in corals,
Genoa, 1579,
steel, gilded silver, turquoises,
l 9⁵/₈, 10³/₄, 12¹/₄ inches

Fig. above
Drinking-vessels representing ostriches,
by Elias Geyer, Leipzig, before 1610,
silver, gilded silver,
ostrich-eggs,
h 18¹/₂, 17¹/₂, 18 inches

Fig. on p. 46
Drinking-vessel representing Daphne,
by Abraham Jamnitzer,
Nuremberg, late 16th cent., silver, largely
gilded, corals, h 26³/₄ inches

Fig. on p. 47
Drinking-vessel representing elephant
with tower-shaped burden, by Urban Wolff,
Nuremberg, before 1600,
gilded silver, mother-of-pearl, emeralds,
rubies, one sapphire, h 20¹/₂ inches

Fig. above
Coconut goblets,
Leipzig, South German, around 1600,
coconuts, gilded silver,
h 12, 13³/₄, 11¹/₄ inches

Fig. at the top of the opposite page
Ostrich-egg goblets,
German, South German, around 1600,
ostrich-eggs, gilded silver
h 16³/₄, 14³/₄, 16³/₄, 18 inches

Fig. at the bottom of the opposite page
Nautilus goblets,
by B. Jamnitzer, T. Wolff, E. Geyer,
Nuremberg, Leipzig, early 17th cent.,
h 13³/₄, 12³/₄, 14¹/₂ inches

49

Fig. above
Drinking-vessels:
cock and hen by F. Hillebrand,
pelican by Ch. Kunad, Nuremberg,
around 1600 and 1609, gilded
silver, nautilus snails,
h 11³/₄, 11¹/₂, 16¹/₄ inches

Fig. on the opposite page
Drinking-vessels representing parrot and
partridge, Nuremberg, around 1600,
the partridge by F. Hillebrand,
gilded silver, mother-of-pearl,
emeralds, rubies,
h 12³/₄, 10³/₄ inches

Goblets consisting of coconuts, ostrich-eggs, exotic sea-shells and sea-snails, and ivory were very much the fashion from the late sixteenth century on throughout the seventeenth. The expensive imports that were used as the bodies of the vessels were of such form and colour that they inspired goldsmiths to think up the most fanciful designs. The vessels served a double purpose: they could be both drunk out of and displayed for ornamentation to testify to the richness of their owners. Naturally enough, they were meant only for those strata of society that felt a need for such testimony, usually court circles, but never anybody less than a patrician. And these circles were most keen on acquiring them; for that was the first golden age of European colonialism. It can be safely assumed that in the riotous, gay festivities that were the custom among all sections of society in those days a

great deal of porcelain was broken; and the expensive porcelain at court was not spared either. Some of the bits left were too valuable to be thrown away because they were likely to be found new uses for. They were therefore deposited in storage facilities of some kind. Bizarre figures were engraved on the snail-shell of the nautilus goblet on the opposite page at the workshop of the Bellekin family in Amsterdam at the beginning of the seventeenth century. The group at the bottom, a dragon with a coral tail and a monkey-like figure riding on his back, is thought to have been made in Nuremberg around 1600 to serve as the bottom structure of some other, unknown vessel. When the Green Vault was given a face-lift in 1724 all the pieces that had got into its storage facilities up until then were used to place lots of magnificent objects on the numerous brackets that were put up. At that time

Fig. below
Drinking-vessels representing
Nereis, sea-unicorn and sea-horse,
by Elias Geyer, Leipzig, before 1610,
h 7 1/8, 7 3/4, 7 3/8 inches

Fig. on the opposite page
Nautilus goblet, first half of the 17th cent.,
parts of the setting by J. H. Köhler,
Dresden, 1724, h 16 1/2 inches

Dresden Court Jeweller Köhler combined the two parts and added an appropriate setting for greater harmony. In addition, he invented the dragon that crowns the new creation.

The Green Vault contains quite a number of works that are made of comparatively cheap materials: wood, bronze, glass and iron. They had been in the Art Chamber for centuries and, when the Green Vault was set up, were put there. The reason is that they are of great artistry and technological finesse. Incidentally, it was never the value of the materials alone that led to the inclusion of an object in the collection; the most important consideration was invariably its artistic and technological perfection.

An example is Archangel Michael defeating Satan, a group made of linden-wood in Southern Germany, presumably in the last few years of the sixteenth century. It resembles Hubert Gerhard's monumental bronze group at the Munich St. Michael Church, even in many details. We do not know, however, who it was made by. But the craftsman must have been one of the great South German artists, for there is no small wood-carved sculpture of this kind that can compare with it in imagination and beauty. The angel in his flying garment, which is pressed against his body, appears to have swooped down on the demon like an eagle from the sky, holding his lance to his enemy's throat. Yet he wields the lance with effortless ease, for he has been sent by Deity, who preordained his victory. It is the great merit of the anonymous artist to have displayed a delicate equilibrium of divine strength and great drama, on the one hand, and divine ease and composure, on the other. The equilibrium is manifest in the entire figure of the militant archangel from his streaming curls down to the tips of his toes, and it is concentrated in the expression of his face. This face is a truly amazing invention.

Fig. on the opposite page
Archangel Michael,
South German, early 17th cent.,
linden-wood, h 24 inches

Fig. on the right
Jewel-cabinet,
by Mattheus Wallbaum,
Augsburg, around 1600,
ebony, silver, partly gilded,
$33^3/_4 \times 21 \times 15^1/_4$ inches

56

Fig. on the opposite page
Bathing Woman,
by Adriaen de Vries (?),
before 1600, bronze,
h 15$^1/_2$ inches

Fig. below
Faun and Nymph,
by Giovanni da Bologna,
Florence, before 1587, bronze,
h 8$^1/_4$ inches

This miner's equipment was made by Samuel Klemm in the town of Freiberg for a big court festival which Elector Johann Georg II once gave in Dresden. Festivals of this kind were of greatest political importance. The equipment is in every detail a copy of the ornamental and symbolic accessories of the holiday costume of Saxon miners. The copy is, of course, much more expensive than the original because the Elector presented himself in it as the Mine-Owner Supreme on the occasion. It bears inscriptions saying that it is made of Saxon silver and Saxon precious stones such as smoky topaz, rock-crystal, garnet and opal. This was one of the not at all rare cases when customs of common people were seized upon by courts, and it also goes to show that mining was of great importance for Saxony.

Since the end of the sixteenth century there were goldsmiths in Saxony whose works were comparable to those made in Nuremberg. David Winkler worked in Freiberg in the early seventeenth century; his Miner's Goblet is one of the best works of his time. Its inscription says that it was made of Saxon silver for the Electoral Foundry at Grünthal in 1625 to serve as what was called a cup of welcome. The lid carries a smelter in work clothes who holds the coat-of-arms of the Saxon electorate in his hands. The rounded wall of the goblet shows scenes related to the smelting of silver ore. Making the reliefs, the master-craftsman took loose guidance from illustrations in Agricola's scientific treatise which explained the fundamentals of contemporary mining. The scenes were embossed on the metal plate with a hammer. The artist's admirable control over the material and his consummate artistry are perfectly easy to see.

Fig. on the opposite page
Parts of the miner's equipment of
Elector Johann Georg II,
by Samuel Klemm, Freiberg, 1675–77

Fig. on p. 63
Three Saxon goblets:
Goblet of Welcome of the Saiger Foundry
at Grünthal (a part of it on p. 62),
by David Winckler, Freiberg (Saxony), 1625,
h 26¹/₄ inches;
Cylindrical Goblet by Valentin Geitner,
Dresden, before 1590, h 21¹/₄ inches;
Aquilegia Goblet by Georg Mond, Dresden
early 17th cent., h 27¹/₂ inches

Fig. above
Gold coin cups,
by Abraham Schwedler,
Dresden, 1635, h 5¹/₂ inches

Fig. on the opposite page
Reverse side of a mirror,
around 1670, gold, enamel,
7¹/₂ × 5³/₄ inches

Most delicate and complex vessels were cut from rock-crystal by Milan master-craftsmen at the end of the sixteenth century, although the material is as hard as granite. Large blocks of it were still found in the Alps in those days. But only few rocks were pure enough and had sufficiently few cracks to be turned into fairly large vessels. Even the crude material was a rarity. The Milan masters used the strength of water when they were cutting them. They even built what were called rock mills, with wheels of amazing proportions whose movement was transferred via several transmissions to a shaft on to which a little wheel was mounted which span at enormous speed. Their art presupposed a profound knowledge of the properties of the material and the latest technological equipment of the time. Rock-crystal was cut against its natural geometrical crystal structure. When cut thin, it tends to break far more easily than glass blown to take the same shape. Therefore all these rock-crystal works are technological and artistic miracles. Even at the time when they were being made they were so expensive that it was justified to give them settings of enamelled gold studded with rubies and emeralds. And the skill of the goldsmiths was in no way inferior to that of the stone-cutters. Only rich dynasties could afford buying such vessels.

Most of the large amount of amber in the Green Vault was made in workshops in the towns of Danzig and Königsberg in the seventeenth and eighteenth centuries. The unyielding material was given highest artistic quality there; it was sawn and cut, coloured and engraved and presumably even pressed. Some of these techniques died out with the families that ran the businesses in which they were used. When the works of art were fairly large—boxes or cabinets—the pieces of amber were usually placed on wooden cores. Since variations of temperature and humidity cause the two materials to contract and expand to varying degrees, layers of paper were glued between them for compensation. But even the best glue will yield after centuries. Additionally, climatic variations make the surface of cut and polished amber porous and cracky. So amber pieces will rapidly age and decay, unless there are restorers on hand who know how to treat the material to prevent that. This is a problem that every museum faces that keeps works of this kind. Our amber collection was sharing the same fate. This is particularly true to say of a large amber cabinet, which suffered heavy damage in World War Two. The collection generally and the cabinet in particular were saved thanks to the friendly help of, and our cooperation with, the Castle Museum in Malbork and the Chair of Restoration Technology of Torún University in the Polish People's Republic.

Fig. above
Drinking-vessels
made of gems, enamelled gold:
vessel with lid, in heliotrope,
gem cut presumably in Prague, around 1600,
setting German, mid-17th cent.,
h 5³/₄ inches;
vessel with lid, in jasper, rock-crystal,
German, third quarter of the 17th cent.,
h 7 inches;
vessel in lapis lazuli,
French, mid-17th cent., h 3¹/₂ inches;
vessel with lid, in jaspagate, presumably
French, early 17th cent., h 7¹/₄ inches

Fig. below
Vessels in rock-crystal,
Milan, around 1580,
gold, emeralds, rubies, enamel,
the bottle from the Sarachi workshop,
h 12¹/₂ inches, h 10³/₄ inches

Fig. on the opposite page
Ewer in lapis lazuli,
by Bernardo Buontalenti (?),
Florence, late 16th cent., h 10³/₄ inches

Fig. above
Drinking-vessels in jasper, agate
and heliotrope, Italian, around 1600,
the third vessel from the left
presumably by J. G. Kobenhaupt,
Stuttgart, first quarter of the 17th cent.,
h 5$^1/_2$, 2$^1/_8$, 3$^3/_8$, 4 inches

Fig. at the top of the opposite page
Rock-crystal goblets in settings from
Freiburg im Breisgau, Nuremberg, Augsburg,
from 1560 till early 17th cent.,
h 10$^3/_4$, 15$^1/_4$, 10, 15$^3/_4$ inches

Fig. at the bottom of the opposite page
Box, double goblet, beaker
in nephrite and serpentine,
German, Zöblitz, Dresden, before 1600 till
around 1660, h 9$^7/_8$, 13, 4$^7/_8$ inches

Fig. on pp. 72–73
Amber cabinet,
Königsberg, before 1742,
23$^1/_4$ × 16$^1/_4$ × 10$^1/_4$ inches

Fig. on pp. 74–75
Turnery pieces in ivory,
Dresden, late 16th cent.,
h 19$^1/_4$ inches (by Jacob Zeller),
14$^1/_2$, 20$^1/_2$ inches (by Jacob Zeller);
h 24, 17$^1/_2$, 22$^3/_4$ inches

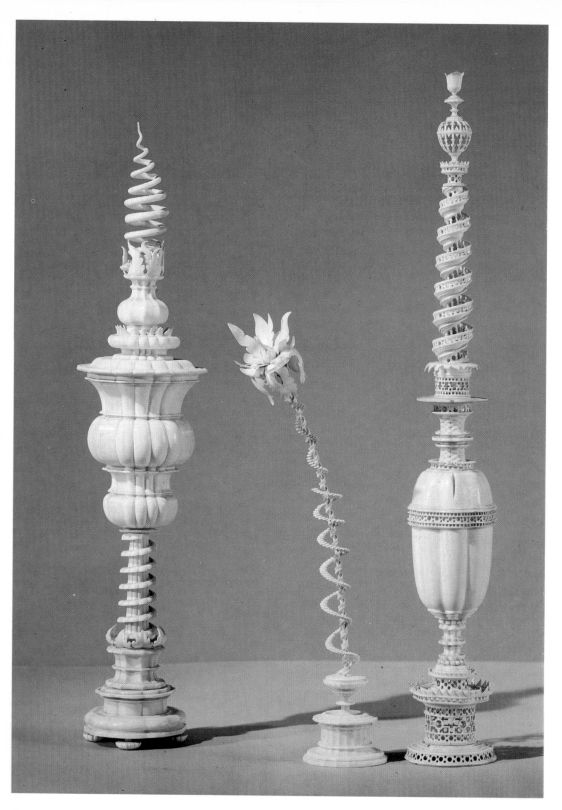

The turnery pieces in ivory are generally believed to be odd and incomprehensible products designed to pander to the eccentricities of princes. This is far from true, although ivory was so expensive that it could be used for turning only at courts. But in the parts of the world that were known at the time it was the only material available that was both flexible and strong enough to allow such pieces to be made. What is of interest to us today is that they were made. One should not forget that they were shaped entirely on turning lathes which were designed at the end of the sixteenth century, and that these lathes, primitive as they may have been by today's standards, were able to move eccentrically in pre-determined curves both on the horizontal and the vertical planes. But a thorough knowledge of mathematics and the latest mechanics, and a good deal of artistic imagination were needed to operate them and make them produce something interesting.

Working these machines, our ancestors in the Renaissance period must have been fascinated by technology for the first time in history. Practically unimaginable shapes, which even the best craftsmen might have needed months to file, saw, cut and polish, could now be made with the help of science and technology at amazing speed with the greatest clarity of line and perfection of cut. There were only few experts who were capable of doing that. They signed and dated their works.

Saxony's electors had their court turners teach them their art and were proud to send their works to rulers who they had made friends with. They had good reasons for taking an interest in the advance of science and technology, reasons that are explained in the first few paragraphs of this Introduction.

Fig. on p. 78
The Farnese Bull,
by Melchior Barthel, Dresden, around 1670,
ivory, wood,
$15^1/_2 \times 13^1/_2 \times 7^1/_2$ inches

Fig. on p. 79
Venus with Mirror,
German, second quarter of the 17th cent.,
ivory, h 12 inches

Fig. on the opposite page
Beaker in ivory,
after Georg Petel,
Strassburg setting of gilded silver,
before the mid-17th cent., h $10^3/_4$ inches

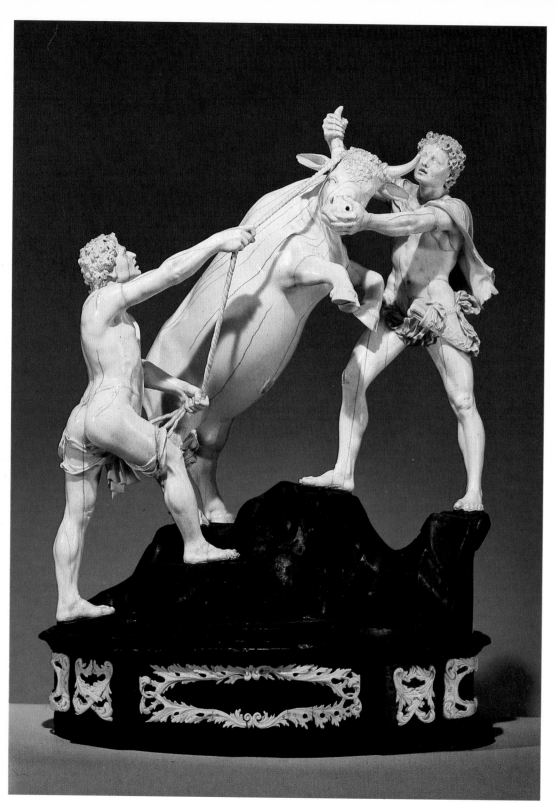

At the beginning of the eighteenth century, when Bavarian sculptor Balthasar Permoser was called to Dresden and Augustus the Strong commissioned works of art on an unprecedented scale, plastic art began to flourish here. Permoser had a perfect command of the traditionally dramatic and expressive language of shape in German plastic art, and he merged it with its opposite, courtly elegance. Since he had this peculiar and highly individual gift, he was capable of an extraordinary variety of artistic expression. He turned tiny bits of ebony and ivory, large trunks of linden-trees, blocks of marble and boulders of sandstone into cheerful putti, strange Africans, graceful young women, grave church fathers, scourged Christ in severest pain, antique gods and impressive portraits. Though different in expression and purpose, these figures have one thing in common: a splendid delicacy of plastic line, which numerous apprentices and assistants of this master adopted and which accounts for the fame of the Dresden sculptors' school of those decades.

The Green Vault has a large number of mini-sculptures. Most of them were made jointly by sculptors and goldsmiths. They all combine the elegance, gracefulness and expressiveness which Permoser started in Dresden's plastic art, with an admirable perfection of plastic detail, whatever the subject dealt with. The famous porcelain designer Kändler was Permoser's grandson and one of his apprentices, and the Green Vault's mini-sculptures, which he knew, were the forerunners of the porcelain figures he made later on.

Fig. above
Beaker and goblet in ivory,
German, 17th cent.,
in settings of gilded silver, enamel,
gems, h 15¹/₄, 21¹/₄ inches

Fig. on pp. 82–83,
Autumn (a part of it on p. 82)
and Spring,
by Balthasar Permoser, Dresden, 1714,
ivory, h 8³/₄ inches each

Some of the most beautiful works of our collection are those which were made jointly by sculptor Permoser and jeweller Dinglinger. They and architect Pöppelmann were the most important artists of Dresden Baroque. Naturally enough, jewellers and sculptors cooperated when works of cabinet-piece dimensions were being made, all of them cheerful, playful and elegant, and solely designed to give delight. To us, it is important that this effect was not confined to the courtiers who these works were intended for, but is also felt by us today, since these works have resisted the ravages of time.

Dinglinger's Diana's Bath with Permosers' ivory goddess of hunting may have been inspired by the transparent rose-coloured and bluish vessel of oriental chalcedony which forms part of the piece. The vessel reproduces something like moonlight, which matches the virgin goddes, who is ornamented with the moon. Dinglinger balanced the vessel on the antlers of a stag's head representing the head of poor hunter Actaeon, who, having seen the goddess bathing, was changed by her into a stag to be torn apart by his own dogs. "Audacity is punished, decency rewarded", says the French inscription at the foot of the vessel.

Fig. above
Nile Barge with Apis Bull
from the Apis Altar,
by J. M. Dinglinger and J. G. Kirchner,
Kehlheim stone, precious stones,
gilded silver,
$5^7/_8 \times 13^1/_4 \times 3^3/_4$ inches

Fig. on the right
Two Moors with Camel, by B. Permoser
and J. M. Dinglinger,
gold, enamel, diamonds, rubies,
ebony, ivory,
Dresden, early 18th cent., h 5 inches

Fig. on p. 86
Diana's Bath
(part of it on p. 87),
cabinet piece by J. M. Dinglinger,
the ivory group by B. Permoser,
gold, silver, enamel, diamonds,
chalcedony, Dresden, 1704, h 15 inches

Fig. on pp. 88–89
Hottentot Couple, by B. Permoser,
Dresden, before 1716,
ivory, gilded silver,
h 7¹/₄ inches

Fig. on the left
Rhinoceros Horn Goblet
with Moor Woman,
by J. M. Dinglinger
and B. Thomae,
Dresden,
between 1700 and 1709,
h 14¹/₂ inches

Fig. on the opposite page
Moor with Emerald Stair,
by J. M. Dinglinger
and B. Permoser,
Dresden,
around 1724, h 25 inches

Fig. below
Knife-Grinder,
the setting by J. H. Köhler,
Dresden, 1708, ivory, glass, gold,
diamonds, rubies, enamel, h 2⅝ inches

Fig. below
Potter,
presumably by an ivory carver of
the Lücke workshop, the setting by
J. H. Köhler, Dresden, around 1710–20,
gold, silver, precious stone, enamel,
varnish, $4^3/_4 \times 3^7/_8 \times 3^7/_8$ inches

Fig. on the opposite page
Time Lifts Sunken Art,
by J. Ch. L. Lücke, Dresden, 1736,
ivory, painted wood,
h (without pedestal) $8^5/_8$ inches

Fig. below
Box for writing utensils
with court jester J. Fröhlich,
presumably by C. A. Lücke der Jüngere,
Dresden, 1731,
ivory, ebony, walnut tree, silver,
gold, precious stones,
$9^1/_8 \times 9^3/_8 \times 6^5/_8$ inches

Fig. below
Lidded goblet and lidded cup,
in ruby glass, presumably Potsdam,
late 17th cent.,
and South German, early 18th cent.,
h 16½, 6½ inches

Fig. on the opposite page
Cup with lid,
by G. Spiller, Potsdam, around 1700,
glass, h 11 inches

Dinglinger, like Permoser, was the leader and founder of an important school. An unknown Swabian journeyman goldsmith, he went to Dresden at the end of the seventeenth century and started what turned out to be a meteorite career. When Augustus the Strong spent the first few years of his kingship exclusively in Warsaw, Dinglinger was the only one of his Dresden court artists to be capable of making new, great and spectacular works of art to add to, and celebrate, the glory of the new crown, since his works were movable: the Gold Coffee-Set, Diana's Bath and sets of jewels. It was he who invented the amusing, lively ornamentation of Dresden Baroque, which one comes across in all works of the period. He was varying contemporary French patterns. This court jeweller, who was a true genius, was the first to keep an eye on what happened on the art scene elsewhere in the world, to make use of elements found in other civilizations—those of East Asia, the classical antiquity and Egypt—and to express ideas typical of the era of Enlightenment. At the same time a few other jewellers worked in Dresden for the court. Outstanding among them was Johann Heinrich Köhler, since he was closest to Dinglinger in liveliness of imagination and elegance of performance. Influenced by this splendid artist, even master-craftsmen who we hardly know of today made marvellous works of art. This great Dresden school of jeweller's art lasted for the entire eighteenth century.

Fig. below
Valuables by J. M. Dinglinger,
Dresden, late 17th cent. till around 1720,
gold, diamonds, enamel: box, ornamental
vase, small phial, steatite box,
h 2³/₄, 6¹/₈, 2⁵/₈, 3⁵/₈ inches

Fig. on the opposite page
Dragon vessel with Medea,
cabinet piece by J. M. Dinglinger,
Dresden, before 1709,
sardonyx, gold, diamonds, enamel,
h 11³/₄ inches

Fig. above,
Parts of the Gold Coffee-Set,
by J. M. Dinglinger, the enamel by his
brother G. F. Dinglinger,
Dresden, 1697–1701,
gold, enamel, diamonds,
h 1$^1/_2$, 8$^1/_8$, 2$^3/_4$ inches

Fig. on the opposite page
Cartouche with
medallion carrying the portrait of
Augustus the Strong, from the cabinet piece
Obeliscus Augustalis,
by J. M. Dinglinger, Dresden, before 1722,
h 8$^7/_8$ inches

Translation of page 102:

Barthold Heinrich Brocke's
Inspection of a Strangely Beautiful
Winter Scenery

A forest of rock-crystal full of diamond twigs
Is on display all over the place.
The whole world has now become
a Dresden green vault,
Since you see nothing but glistening
brilliants
And quivering cut diamonds
Far and wide.

From: Earthly Pleasures in God,
Hamburg 1732

Fig. on pp. 104–105
Keeping Great State at the Delhi Court on
the Birthday of Grand Mogul Aurungzebe
(part of it on page 103), by J. M. Dinglinger
and his brothers, Dresden, 1701–08,
gold, silver, partly gilded, enamel,
precious stones, $22^3/_4 \times 56 \times 45$ inches

Barthold Heinrich Brockes
Betrachtung
einer sonderbar schönen Winterlandschaft

Ein
Wald von Bergkristall voll diamantner Reiser
sind überall zur Schau gestellt.
Ein Dresdnisch grün Gewölb
war ietzt die ganze Welt;
weil nichts als spielende Brillianten,
als schütternde geschliffene Diamanten,
so weit man sah, zu sehn.

Aus: Irdisches Vergnügen in Gott, Hamburg 1732

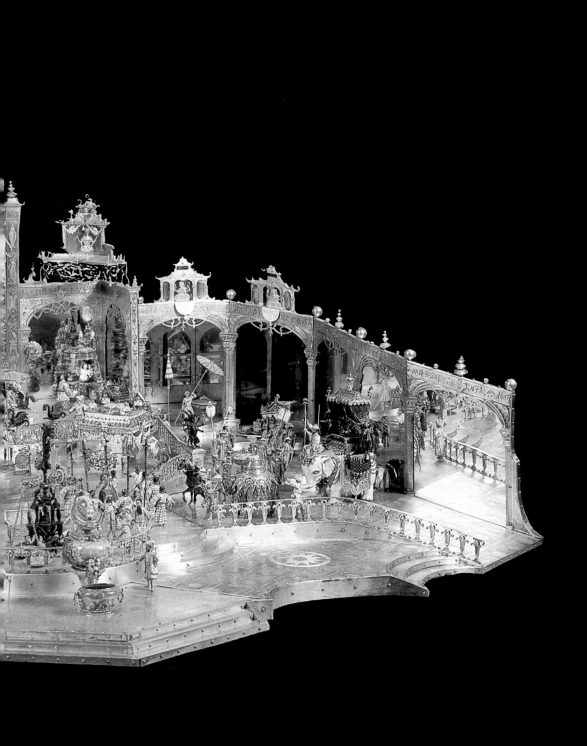

Fig. on p. 106
Pyx-shaped clock,
pocket watch by J. Droynot, Poitiers,
converted into a pendulum-clock by
J. H. Köhler in Dresden in 1725;
gilded silver, precious stones, cameos,
one pearl, h 9 inches

Fig. on p. 107
Hubertus Clock,
French clock by J. H. Köhler
and J. G. Graupner, Dresden, after 1720,
gold, gilded silver, precious stones,
enamel, h 14$^1/_4$ inches

Fig. above
Halberdier,
presumably by J. H. Köhler, Dresden,
before 1725;
Joshua and Caleb,
presumably Dresden, early 18th cent.,
gold, precious stones, pearls,
enamel, gilded silver,
h 4, 5 inches

Fig. on the opposite page
Little Altar with St. Joseph,
by J. H. Köhler, Dresden, around 1730,
gilded silver, corals, precious stones,
enamel, h 11$^3/_4$ inches

The Green Vault has the largest collection of a special group of jeweller's sculptures for which there is no appropriate name. These sculptures are small figures composed of pearls, precious stones and enamelled gold. The invention was usually stimulated by a misshapen pearl. All these figures reveal sculptural skill and have an astounding power of expression. Although of very valuable material, they do not appear ostentatious and florid, which shows that the jewellers who made them had great ability and subtle taste. Some old art collections contain a very few similar pieces; they are usually called Dresden works. But only few of them are as well done as all the pieces are which we have; they are contemporary imitations. Their superb qualities notwithstanding, these many pieces of the Green Vault have not as yet been investigated. Eighteenth-century inventories mention Jean Gerardet, a Huguenot living in Berlin, and a certain Ferbecq from Frankfort on the Main, who seems to have been a mere trader, though. Other works are ascribed to the Dresden Court Jeweller Köhler. But Dinglinger's workshop is also likely to have been involved.

Fig. above
Three small grotesque figures:
Merry Vintager, Rollicking Cook,
Dancing Dwarf,
presumably Dresden, early 18th cent.,
h 3¹/₈, 4³/₄, 3¹/₈ inches

Fig. on the opposite page
Three small grotesque figures:
"by Gerardet in Berlin" and presumably
Dresden, early 18th cent., Baroque pearls,
gold, gilded silver, precious stones,
ivory, enamel, h 4, 4³/₈, 3¹/₂ inches

Fig. on p. 112
Five snuff-boxes,
Dresden, presumably Paris and English,
around 1740–70, enamel, chalcedony,
mother-of-pearl, gold,
b 3¹/₂, 2⁷/₈, 2¹/₂, 2⁵/₈, 2⁷/₈ inches

Fig. on p. 113
Three snuff-boxes,
by J. Ch. Neuber,
Dresden, around 1770–80,
gold, Saxon gems,
dia 3, 3⁵/₈, 3³/₈ inches

The nine jewel sets of the Green Vault, together with the jewellery from the sixteenth and seventeenth centuries, are the greatest historical jewel treasure in Europe. The earliest sets were made for Augustus the Strong; they include the Sapphire Set and the Cornelian Set, either of which Dinglinger's workshop helped to make, and the Diamond-Facet Set and the Tortoise-Shell Set, which were made later. But most of the jewellery of the other sets were made in later decades of the eighteenth century. A large number of the jewellery were changed in line with the changing requirements of fashion in subsequent decades. Even in the 1820's most of the fairly large brilliants were broken out of the Tortoise-Shell Set, the artistically most valuable set in the possession of Augustus the Strong, to be added to the Brilliant Set. This was a foolish and belated thing to do; for jewel sets of this kind had come into fashion with the emergence of absolutism, and after absolutism was dealt the death-blow in the French revolution in 1789, they could not be worn any more. They had been political jewellery used by the dynasty of a sovereign to symbolize their claim to total power. They were ideally suited for the purpose: getting a set of this kind together required not only tapping the financial resources of a whole country for the purchase of the stones needed, but also inheriting most of them from one's ancestors, because precious stones of this magnitude and quality were at no time offered on the market in such quantities. Therefore this jewellery manifested a claim to power that was rooted even in history. What we are left with today is the art of the jewellers and the miracle of colour embodied by these minerals, which the consummate artistry of cutters made sparkle. Nowhere in the nature of this country will you find a green like that of the Emerald Set,

a green concentrated almost to the point of blackness and of immaculate purity. Ever since it was acquired more than 200 years ago, the 41-carat Dresden Green Brilliant in the Brilliant Set has remained unique. Nowhere will you see such beautiful yellow brilliants as those in the rings of the Brilliant Pearl Set.

So, this jewellery expressed a claim to emperorship. But there are no crowns, sceptres and mounds among them, although they were available. Since these luxurious heavy symbols of state power were used only once, at the coronation, stones were set on them in a way which allowed their easy removal. The large, almost conical sapphire of the Sapphire Set, e.g., was mounted at the top of the crown of Augustus III as the King of Poland; the crown is now in the Warsaw National Museum. The sapphire, like the other large stones, was replaced by glass- paste. The idea was that the magnificent stones should be worn, rather than locked up in some safe. So the stones adorned their wearers when stately receptions were being held and gay festivities were taking place at the Zwinger. The criticism that we have to make is that all this was paid for by the common people, whose hardships were regarded as a normal fact of life under absolutism, as is shown by the large number of ornamental beggar's figures in porcelain, ivory, gold, and precious stones.

Now, after so many social changes, these pieces of jewellery have retained what is most important about them: they are miracles of nature, of cutter's art and of jeweller's art. And we have been doing our utmost to bring them as close to the eyes of visitors as possible and illumine them as correctly as possible.

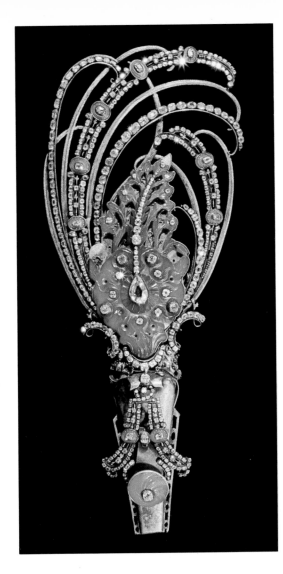

Fig. on p. 116
Parts of the Sapphire Set:
hat-brim, Order of the Polish White
Eagle (by J. M. Dinglinger), sword and
sword-belt ornaments
(by J. M. Dinglinger), unset sapphire,
Dresden, around 1700–21

Fig. on p. 117
Parts of the Diamond-Facet Set:
sword, Star of the Polish White Eagle,
Order of the Golden Fleece
with Brazilian topazes
(by A. J. Pallard, before 1756),
hat-brim, large buckle; Dresden, 18th cent.

Fig. on p. 118
Parts of the Ruby Set:
Order and Star of the Polish White
Eagle, snuff-box (by D. Gouers, Paris,
around 1730), sword, four buckles,
shirt-button; Dresden,
second quarter of the 18th cent.

Fig. on p. 119
Parts of the Emerald Set:
hunting-knife (by J. M. Dinglinger,
first decade of the 18th cent.),
Order of the Polish White Eagle,
hat-brim, buckle, sword
(by J. F. Dinglinger, 1737),
shirt-button; Dresden,
first third of the 18th cent.

Fig. on p. 120
Parts of the Brilliant Set:
sword, had agraffe, shoulder slip-knot
with the Saxon White Brilliant
weighing 48⁴/₈ carats, hat agraffe with the
Green Brilliant weighing 41 carats,
ornament; Dresden, mid-18th cent.

Fig. above
Aigrette
from the Cornelian Set,
design by J. M. Dinglinger,
Dresden, around 1719

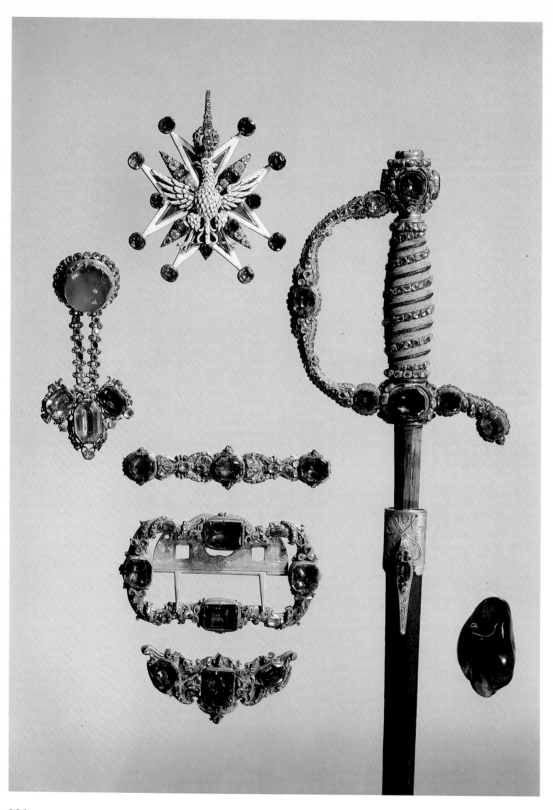